Uncomplicated AIDA Method: Convert Attention into Sales

Copyright © 2024 Reginaldo Osnildo
All rights reserved.

PRESENTATION

INTRODUCTION TO THE AIDA METHOD: THE PURCHASING JOURNEY REVEALED

CAPTURING ATTENTION: FIRST STEPS TO ENGAGEMENT

AKINING INTEREST: KEEPING THE CUSTOMER ENGAGED

CREATING DESIRE: THE HEART OF CONVERSION

DRIVING TO ACTION: EFFECTIVE CLOSING STRATEGIES

PERSONALIZATION IN THE AIDA PROCESS: MAKING THE CUSTOMER FEEL UNIQUE

OVERCOMING BARRIERS: AIDA IN PRACTICE

USING DIGITAL TOOLS TO POWER AIDA

AIDA IN DIFFERENT CHANNELS: ONLINE AND OFFLINE

RESOURCES TO DEEPEN YOUR KNOWLEDGE

30-DAY ACTION PLAN: IMPLEMENTING AIDA INTO YOUR SALES PROCESS

REGINALDO OSNILDO

PRESENTATION

Welcome to "**Uncomplicated AIDA Method: Convert Attention into Sales**", the definitive guide that will transform the way you see and apply sales and marketing strategies in your daily life. If you are a salesperson or marketer looking to not just meet but exceed your goals, this book is tailor-made for you.

We live in a world where consumer attention has never been more competitive. Constant technological innovations and the avalanche of content available online make the challenge of standing out even greater. This is where this book comes in: to be your beacon in this storm of information, offering clarity and direction. Throughout these pages, you will be introduced to the AIDA method - ATTENTION, INTEREST, DESIRE, ACTION - a classic framework that remains remarkably relevant in our digital age, helping you guide your customer through each step of the sales funnel with precision. and effectiveness.

We're not just here to revisit theories; Let's take a deep dive into how these concepts can be adapted and applied in the current context, ensuring you leave not just with knowledge, but with an arsenal of strategies ready to be implemented. This book is the result of extensive research, but also of real experiences adapted to meet the needs of the current market. Each chapter has been carefully crafted to provide not just theory, but also practical examples, applicable tips, and valuable insights that you can use to optimize your sales and marketing strategies.

WHAT CAN YOU EXPECT?

- **Detailed introduction to the AIDA method**, simplifying each step of the purchasing process and showing how you can use this knowledge to create more effective strategies.

- **Creative and innovative strategies** to capture customer attention, spark interest, create desire and, ultimately, induce action.

- **Personalization techniques** to make each customer feel

unique, increasing the chances of conversion at each stage of the process.

- **Practical advice** to overcome common barriers, using digital tools to enhance your actions and adapting the AIDA method to different channels, both online and offline.

This book is an invitation for you to dive headfirst into the world of sales and marketing, armed with the knowledge and tools necessary to stand out. With each chapter, you'll discover new ways to engage your customers and, more importantly, convert them. And at the end of this journey, you will not only have absorbed a significant amount of knowledge, but you will also be ready to apply these strategies and see tangible results.

Ready to transform attention into sales in an uncomplicated way? So, turn the page and start this journey. The next step, **"INTRODUCTION TO THE AIDA METHOD: THE PURCHASING JOURNEY REVEALED"**, awaits you with essential insights to start applying now. Let's together unlock the potential of your business and take your sales and marketing strategies to a new level.

Yours sincerely

Reginaldo Osnildo

INTRODUCTION TO THE AIDA METHOD: THE PURCHASING JOURNEY REVEALED

Welcome to the first step of your transformation in sales and marketing strategies. This chapter is dedicated to unveiling the AIDA method, a concept that, despite being created in the distant year 1898 by Elias St. Elmo Lewis, remains incredibly relevant and effective in the modern consumer's purchasing journey. AIDA is an acronym for ATTENTION, INTEREST, DESIRE and ACTION, and serves as a roadmap to guide potential customers through each phase of the buying process.

A - Attention: The first step is to capture the attention of your target audience. In a world bombarded by information, making your product or service stand out is crucial. At this stage, creativity and visibility are your best tools.

I - Interest: Once you have the consumer's attention, the next step is to maintain and deepen that interest. This is done by highlighting the aspects of your product or service that are most relevant and appealing to your audience. This is where you start to create a more meaningful connection with the potential customer.

D - Desire: Interest is not the same as desire. Desire comes when the prospect not only understands the benefits of the product or service, but also internalizes them, visualizing how they could improve their life or solve a specific problem.

A – Action: The final stage is where you encourage the customer to take a specific action, whether that's making a purchase, signing up for a free trial, or requesting more information. Calls to action (CTAs) are vital here to convert that interest and desire into tangible action.

APPLYING AIDA TODAY

You may be wondering: how can such an old concept still be relevant in the digital age? The answer lies in the universality of the consumer journey. Despite changes in channels and technologies, the fundamental process by which people make purchasing decisions remains the same. However, to be effective today, it is essential to adapt and update AIDA strategies for the current context.

ATTENTION IN THE DIGITAL WORLD

Capturing attention today means understanding where your target audience spends their time and how they consume information. This can be on social media, search engines, or through video content. The important thing is to create content that not only attracts attention, but is also valuable and relevant to your audience.

INTEREST WITH VALUE

Maintaining customer interest is more challenging than ever. It's crucial to provide ongoing value through educational content, entertainment or solutions to common problems. Well-constructed brand stories and personalized content can be extremely effective here.

DESIRE THROUGH CONNECTION

Creating desire is creating an emotional connection. Use customer success stories, product demonstrations, or lifetime visualizations to help potential customers see themselves benefiting from your product or service. Making the product tangible, even if only in the customer's imagination, is key.

SIMPLIFIED ACTION

The action must be easy and free from obstacles. This means having a simple purchasing process, flexible payment options, and guarantees that remove perceived risk. A good CTA is clear, convincing and takes the customer directly to the desired next step.

WHERE DO WE GO FROM HERE?

Now that you have a solid understanding of the AIDA method

and its relevance today, it's time to dive into the specific strategies you can apply to capture your audience's attention. In the next chapter, " **CAPTURING ATTENTION: FIRST STEPS TO ENGAGEMENT** ", we'll explore creative and innovative techniques that not only capture attention but also lay the foundation for a lasting relationship with your customers.

Get ready to unlock the power of attention in your sales and marketing strategies. Let's turn theory into practice and begin the journey to convert attention into sales in an effective and impactful way. Turn the page and start turning potential into reality.

CAPTURING ATTENTION: FIRST STEPS TO ENGAGEMENT

In today's world, where every second counts and the competition for attention has never been so fierce, capturing the consumer's gaze is the first and, perhaps, the biggest challenge of any sales and marketing strategy. In this chapter, we'll explore how you can effectively capture this sought-after attention, turning passive observers into active participants in your brand's story.

UNDERSTAND YOUR AUDIENCE

The first step to capturing attention is to deeply understand who your target audience is. What are your interests? Where do they spend their time online? What problems are they trying to solve? A clear understanding of your audience not only directs your message to the right people, it also helps you personalize that message to resonate with them on a deeper level.

THE POWER OF VISUALS

In an era dominated by social media, visual content has never been more important. Striking images, engaging videos, and eye-catching designs have an unparalleled ability to stop screens from scrolling and grab attention. Invest in high-quality visual content that highlights your product or service in creative and unexpected ways.

BE USEFUL

Offering value from the first contact is an infallible strategy for capturing and keeping attention. This can be done through educational content such as blogs, e-books, webinars or tutorial videos that not only inform but also solve problems for your target audience. By positioning yourself as a source of knowledge and solutions, you not only capture attention but also build trust.

CREATE ATTRACTIVE TITLES

In the sea of online content, a catchy title is like a beacon for lost ships. It should be able to grab attention and provoke enough curiosity to make someone stop and want to know more. Use numbers, questions, teasers, or bold statements to make your headlines irresistible.

USE SOCIAL MEDIA TO YOUR ADVANTAGE

Social media is fertile ground for capturing attention, but it requires a strategic approach. Knowing the peculiarities of each platform and adapting your content for each of them can significantly increase your reach and engagement. Furthermore, using resources such as relevant hashtags, stories and lives can amplify your visibility and attract more eyes to your brand.

NARRATIVE IS KEY

Stories connect people. Using narrative to tell the story of your product or service, how it was created, the problems it solves or the lives it changed, can be extremely powerful. People remember stories long after they forget statistics or facts, so use this power to your advantage.

AUTHENTICITY GENERATES CONNECTION

In a world of constant sales and marketing, authenticity stands out. Be truthful in your messages and the stories you tell. Showing behind the scenes, sharing challenges and successes, and maintaining a consistent and genuine voice will help create an emotional connection with your audience, making your brand more memorable.

PREPARING THE LAND FOR INTEREST

Capturing attention is just the beginning. The real challenge begins with maintaining that attention and transforming it into genuine interest. In the next chapter, " **AKINING INTEREST: KEEPING THE CUSTOMER ENGAGED** ", we'll dive into strategies for keeping your audience engaged, interested, and eager for more information about your product or service. You will learn how to use the interest sparked here to build a solid path toward desire and, ultimately, action.

Get ready to turn captured attention into lasting interest. This is the next step on your journey to converting attention into sales, creating a customer base that is not just interested, but truly engaged with your brand. Let's go together in this?

AKINING INTEREST: KEEPING THE CUSTOMER ENGAGED

Once you've captured your audience's attention, the next big challenge is turning that brief moment of focus into deep, sustained interest. This chapter is dedicated to strategies that not only keep your audience engaged but also increase their interest in your product or service, encouraging them to want to learn more and eventually move toward a purchasing decision.

EDUCATE YOUR AUDIENCE

Education is a powerful tool for maintaining customer interest. Through content that informs, teaches and adds value, you can help your audience better understand your sector, your product and how it can solve their problems or satisfy their needs. Blogs, e-books, webinars and tutorial videos are excellent ways to share knowledge and keep your audience interested.

COMMUNICATE BENEFITS, NOT JUST FEATURES

Potential customers want to know how your product or service can improve their lives. Instead of just focusing on technical features, highlight the real benefits users will get. For example, instead of saying that a smartphone has 128GB of storage, explain how this space can store thousands of photos, videos and applications, simplifying the user's life.

INTERACT AND ENGAGE

Interaction is key to keeping interest alive. Use social media, emails and chats to talk directly to your audience, answer their questions and listen to their feedback. Creating a community around your brand where customers feel heard and valued can turn initial interest into long-term loyalty.

USE STORYTELLING

Stories have the power to engage people on an emotional level. Sharing customer success stories, the process behind creating your product, or even challenges you faced along the way can make your brand more relatable and increase audience interest.

People are naturally drawn to narratives that stir emotions, so use that to your advantage.

DEMONSTRATIONS AND SOCIAL PROOF

One of the best ways to increase interest is to show your product in action. Demos, free trials, samples or virtual tours allow customers to try your product before purchasing, significantly increasing interest. Additionally, include reviews, testimonials, and case studies as social proof to reinforce trust and interest in your product.

CUSTOMIZE THE EXPERIENCE

In a world saturated with generic content, personalization can make your brand stand out. Use data and insights to deliver personalized recommendations, content and offers that align with your audience's individual interests and needs. Personalization not only increases interest but also strengthens the connection with your brand.

KEEP NEW

Keeping your product, service or content updated and bringing new features regularly can reignite and maintain your audience's interest. Whether through new product launches, feature updates or fresh, relevant content, newness encourages customers to stay engaged with your brand.

ADVANCED TOWARDS DESIRE

Sparking and maintaining interest is crucial, but it's only part of the journey. In the next chapter, " **CREATING DESIRE: THE HEART OF CONVERSION** ," we'll explore how you can turn this sustained interest into a burning desire for your product or service. We will set the stage for this interest to evolve to the next stage, where customers are ready to act based on their emotions and perceptions about the value you offer.

Be ready to dive even deeper into the techniques that not only capture your customers' minds but also win their hearts. Let's turn interest into desire together, moving your customers closer and closer to the final purchasing action.

CREATING DESIRE: THE HEART OF CONVERSION

Transforming your customers' interest into desire is an art and a science. At this stage, the goal is to make your customers not just want, but feel like they need, your product or service. Here, we'll explore effective strategies for creating that deep desire, paving the way to the final purchasing action.

APPEAL TO EMOTIONS

Desire is fueled by emotions. To create a deep desire for your product or service, you need to emotionally connect with your audience. This can be done through storytelling, images that provoke feelings, or messages that resonate with customers' values and aspirations. Show how your product can transform the customer's life, bringing happiness, relief, security or any other emotion that your product promises to deliver.

HIGHLIGHT EXCLUSIVITY

People desire what is perceived as exclusive or limited. Highlight the uniqueness of your product or service, emphasizing any aspect that differentiates it from the competition. This may include innovative design, unique functionality, limited availability, or access to an exclusive community. The feeling of having something unique can transform interest into desire.

POWERFUL DEMONSTRATIONS

Seeing is believing, and nothing creates desire like visual proof that your product works wonderfully. Investing in product demos, before and after videos, and in-depth case studies can do wonders for convincing potential customers of the real, tangible value your product or service can bring to their lives.

REINFORCEMENT OF SOCIAL PROOF

The opinion of others has a significant impact on desire. Including positive reviews, customer testimonials and success stories in your communication can reinforce desire, showing that other people not only wanted it, but are satisfied and happy with the purchase decision. Social proof is a powerful persuasion tool that can drive desire and trust in your offering.

CREATE URGENCY

The desire can be intensified by the feeling of urgency. Limited-time offers, countdowns or limited stock are tactics that can make customers act quickly so they don't miss out on the opportunity. The key is to communicate that taking action now is essential to ensuring the value your product or service provides.

CUSTOMIZATION AND RECOMMENDATION

Personalization elevates desire by making the customer feel like your offering is tailor-made for them. Use customer data and preferences to personalize recommendations, offers and messages. The feeling that a solution was created specifically to meet your needs can transform moderate interest into burning desire.

SENSORY ENGAGEMENT

Take advantage of all your senses to create an immersive experience around your product or service. This can be challenging in the digital environment, but not impossible. Use rich descriptions, vivid images, engaging videos, and interactive experiences to engage the senses and make the desire for your product or service undeniable.

PREPARING FOR ACTION

Creating desire is the prelude to the final and most crucial step: action. In the next chapter, " **DRIVING TO ACTION: EFFECTIVE CLOSING STRATEGIES** ", we'll focus on how to convert that desire into concrete purchasing decisions. Let's explore best practices for encouraging your customers to take the last step, using effective calls to action and closing strategies that turn interest and desire into real sales.

Be prepared to learn how to seal the deal, ensuring that the carefully cultivated desire in your customers translates into action. Let's make the transition from desire to decision together, closing the AIDA cycle successfully and effectively.

DRIVING TO ACTION: EFFECTIVE CLOSING STRATEGIES

After successfully awakening your customers' attention, interest, and desire, the final step in the AIDA process is to move them to action. This chapter is dedicated to turning fervent desire into concrete purchasing decisions, using closing strategies that not only encourage but also facilitate action on the part of customers.

CLEAR AND CONVINCING CALLS TO ACTION

An effective call to action (CTA) is crucial to enticing customers to take the next step. Your CTA should be clear, direct, and communicate exactly what you want the customer to do, whether that's make a purchase, sign up for a newsletter, or request more information. Use action verbs and language that inspires urgency or benefit to motivate an immediate response.

SIMPLIFY THE PURCHASE PROCESS

One of the biggest barriers to action is a complicated or time-consuming purchasing process. Analyze and optimize the customer's path to purchase by removing any unnecessary obstacles. This can include simplifying forms, offering multiple payment options, and ensuring your website or e-commerce platform is fast, secure, and easy to navigate.

LIMITED TIME OFFERS

Creating a sense of urgency through limited-time offers is a proven tactic for driving action. Special offers, discounts, and exclusive bonuses available for a limited time only encourage customers to act quickly so they don't miss out.

GUARANTEES AND SOCIAL PROOF

Offering guarantees, such as money back within a specified period or satisfaction guarantees, can reduce perceived risk and encourage action. Additionally, highlighting social proof, such as customer testimonials and positive ratings, reinforces trust in your offering and motivates customers to join others who have already made a purchasing decision.

PERSONALIZATION IN OFFERS

Personalization can be a significant differentiator in your closing strategies. Personalized offers, based on customers' preferences and past behavior, demonstrate that you understand their specific needs, increasing the chances of conversion.

FREE DEMONSTRATIONS AND TRIALS

Allowing customers to try your product or service before purchasing can be a powerful motivator for action. Free trials, samples or hands-on demonstrations reduce uncertainty and allow customers to see for themselves the value of your offering.

TRACKING AND CART RECOVERY

Don't give up on customers who show interest but hesitate at the last minute. Follow-up strategies, such as cart recovery emails or special offers for wishlist items, can reignite interest and encourage completion of the purchase.

ADVANCING BEYOND ACTION

Completing a sale is not the end of the journey with your customer; It's just the beginning of a relationship that can generate repeat business and valuable referrals. In the next chapter, " **PERSONALIZATION IN THE AIDA PROCESS: MAKING THE CUSTOMER FEEL UNIQUE** ", we'll explore how to continue to engage your customers in meaningful ways by personalizing their post-purchase experience for long-term loyalty and satisfaction.

Be ready to learn how personalization not just during but also after the sales process can transform satisfied customers into loyal advocates for your brand, perpetuating a virtuous cycle of engagement and conversion.

PERSONALIZATION IN THE AIDA PROCESS: MAKING THE CUSTOMER FEEL UNIQUE

The digital age has transformed the way we interact with brands and products, raising customer expectations for personalization. A personalized approach not only amplifies the effectiveness of each stage of the AIDA method, but also strengthens the relationship with the client, making them feel unique and valued. In this chapter, we'll explore how to integrate personalization into each step of the AIDA process to enrich the customer experience and strengthen brand loyalty.

ATTENTION: CUSTOM TARGETING

The personalized journey starts with capturing the customer's attention. Use demographic, behavioral, and navigational data to segment your audience and create messages and offers that directly resonate with the specific interests and needs of different groups. Analytics tools and marketing automation platforms are essential for identifying patterns and preferences, allowing you to adjust your campaigns to attract attention more effectively.

INTEREST: CUSTOMIZED CONTENT

After capturing attention, keep the customer engaged with personalized content. This can include targeted emails, product recommendations based on past purchases or website navigation, and blog content that addresses specific questions for segments of your audience. The key is to show that you understand and care about each customer's unique interests, providing value and building an ongoing relationship.

WISH: TAILORED OFFERS

Turning interest into desire requires an even deeper understanding of customer preferences. Use the data collected to personalize offers, highlighting how your products or services can meet your customers' specific needs or solve particular problems. Personalization here can include special offers, personalized packages, or exclusive previews, all designed to make the customer feel like the offer was made especially for them.

ACTION: SIMPLIFIED SHOPPING EXPERIENCE

When the customer is ready to take action, personalization can simplify and enrich the shopping experience. This includes personalized checkout, which remembers payment and delivery preferences, post-purchase offers based on purchase history, and customer support that recognizes the customer and their past interactions with the brand. This approach not only facilitates the purchase action, but also reinforces the feeling of being valued and understood.

AFTER-SALES: CONTINUOUS COMMUNICATION

Personalization doesn't end with purchase. After-sales is a golden opportunity to continue building the relationship. This can include personalized follow-up, customized after-sales support, and re-engagement offers based on specific customer interests. Maintaining relevant and personalized communication after purchase increases satisfaction, loyalty and chances of repurchase.

USING TECHNOLOGY TO PERSONALIZE

Technology is an essential ally in customizing the AIDA process. CRM, data analytics, artificial intelligence and marketing automation platforms are key tools for collecting, analyzing and acting on customer data effectively. They allow you to not only customize at scale, but also continually adjust and refine your strategies to better meet your customers' evolving needs.

LOOKING TO THE FUTURE

Implementing personalization at every step of the AIDA process is not just a strategy for improving conversions; It is an investment in the future of your relationship with customers. In the next chapter, " **OVERCOMING BARRIERS: AIDA IN PRACTICE** ," we'll explore how to overcome common challenges and effectively implement these strategies in the real world, ensuring your approach to AIDA is always aligned with customer expectations and market trends.

Be ready to turn insights into actions that not only capture attention, but also build lasting relationships, making each customer feel truly unique and valued at every stage of their journey.

OVERCOMING BARRIERS: AIDA IN PRACTICE

Implementing the AIDA method, while effective, can face numerous challenges and barriers in today's dynamic sales and marketing environment. This chapter covers practical strategies for overcoming these obstacles, ensuring that you can apply the AIDA method efficiently and effectively in your marketing campaigns and sales efforts.

IDENTIFYING AND OVERCOMING BARRIERS IN CARE

In the ATTENTION stage, the main barrier is market noise. With so many brands competing for the attention of the same audience, standing out becomes a challenge.

Strategies:

- **Precise targeting:** Use demographic, behavioral and psychographic data to refine your target audience, ensuring your messages reach the people most likely to be interested in what you offer.

- **Valuable content marketing:** Create content that is not only relevant, but also valuable and useful to your audience. This may include guides, tutorials, and case studies that address specific problems or interests.

- **Use of paid media:** Investing in paid advertising on platforms where your target audience spends time can help cut through the noise, especially when targeted correctly.

OVERCOMING INTEREST CHALLENGES

Maintaining an audience's interest once you've captured their attention can be challenging, especially with online attention spans decreasing.

Strategies:

- **Interactive engagement:** Use tools such as quizzes, polls and games to engage your audience in an interactive way, keeping interest alive.

- **Direct communication:** Personalized emails and direct messages on social media can help build a more personal relationship and maintain interest over time.

TRANSFORMING INTEREST INTO DESIRE

The transition from interest to desire is crucial and requires a deep understanding of your audience's motivations and needs.

Strategies:

- **Demos and testimonials:** Showing your product or service in action, along with testimonials from satisfied customers, can turn curious interest into passionate desire.

- **Personalized offers:** Use personalization to create offers that speak directly to the customer's individual needs and desires.

MAKING ACTION EASIER

The last step, inducing action, may encounter resistance in the form of hesitation or friction in the purchasing process.

Strategies:

- **Simplifying the checkout process:** Make sure the purchasing process is as simple and straightforward as possible, minimizing unnecessary steps and making it easier to complete the purchase.

- **Clear guarantees and return policies:** Offer strong guarantees and a clear return policy to reduce perceived risk and encourage action.

OVERCOMING BARRIERS WITH CONTINUOUS FEEDBACK AND ADJUSTMENTS

A crucial component to overcoming barriers at any stage of AIDA is continuous feedback and a willingness to adjust your strategies.

- **Data collection and analysis:** Use data from customer interactions, campaign feedback, and performance analytics to understand where barriers are emerging.

- **A/B Testing:** Regularly perform A/B testing on your campaigns to understand what works best and adapt your strategies accordingly.

LOOKING AHEAD

The practical application of the AIDA method requires flexibility, innovation and a continuous commitment to adapting to market changes and customer needs. In the next chapter, " **USING DIGITAL TOOLS TO POWER AIDA** ", we'll explore how digital and technological tools can be leveraged to amplify the impact of each step of AIDA, helping you achieve your marketing and sales goals more effectively.

Get ready to dive into the technologies and platforms that can transform your approach to AIDA, ensuring you're equipped to meet the challenges of modern marketing and make the most of every customer engagement opportunity.

USING DIGITAL TOOLS TO POWER AIDA

In today's highly digitized and constantly evolving marketing environment, the strategic use of digital tools is critical to maximizing the impact of the AIDA method. This chapter explores the technologies and platforms that can be used at each stage of AIDA, helping you capture attention, maintain interest, create desire, and drive action more efficiently and effectively.

TOOLS TO CAPTURE ATTENTION

The battle for consumer attention is fierce, and digital tools can be valuable allies to stand out.

- **Paid advertising on social media and search:** Platforms like **Google Ads** and **Facebook Ads** allow for precise targeting and delivery of messages directly to users most likely to be interested in your product or service.

- **SEO (Search Engine Optimization):** Tools like **SEMrush** and **Ahrefs** can help optimize your content for search engines, increasing organic visibility and attracting relevant traffic to your website.

MAINTAINING INTEREST WITH CONTENT

Content is king in maintaining customer interest. Use platforms and tools to create and distribute content that engages and informs your target audience.

- **Content management platforms (CMS): WordPress** and **HubSpot** are examples of systems that facilitate the creation, management and optimization of content for different channels.

- **Marketing automation:** Tools like **Mailchimp** and **Marketo** allow you to automate email marketing campaigns, keeping your audience engaged with personalized and relevant content.

CREATING DESIRE WITH PERSONALIZATION

Personalization is essential to transform interest into desire. Digital tools can help personalize the user experience by showing how your product or service fits seamlessly into their lives.

- **Customer Data Platforms (CDP):** Tools like **Segment** and **Tealium** collect and organize customer data into a single view, enabling advanced segmentation and messaging personalization.

- **Content recommendation and personalization:** Tools like **Optimizely** and **Adobe Target** allow you to personalize user experiences on the website or in apps, increasing relevance and desire for the product.

DRIVING TO ACTION WITH EASE

Making it easier for customers to take action is crucial to converting interest and desire into sales.

- **E-commerce platforms: Shopify** and **Magento** offer robust solutions for creating optimized online shopping experiences, simplifying the checkout process to reduce cart abandonment.

Conversion Rate Optimization) tools : Hotjar and **Crazy Egg** provide insights into user behavior on your website, allowing you to optimize pages for conversion, highlighting CTAs and simplifying user journeys.

INTEGRATING TOOLS FOR A COHESIVE STRATEGY

The key to maximizing AIDA's impact in the digital environment is to integrate these tools into a cohesive strategy. This means ensuring that each tool and platform is used in a way that complements and reinforces the others, creating a smooth and persuasive customer journey that smoothly guides the consumer from one AIDA step to the next.

As we move towards " **AIDA IN DIFFERENT CHANNELS: ONLINE**

AND OFFLINE ", it is crucial to understand how these digital tools integrate and complement offline strategies, ensuring an omnichannel marketing approach that reaches the consumer wherever they are. This balance between digital and physical is essential to creating truly effective marketing and sales campaigns.

Get ready to explore how to harmonize your online and offline strategies, using the best of both worlds to capture attention, engage, create desire and drive action across a variety of contexts and customer touchpoints.

AIDA IN DIFFERENT CHANNELS: ONLINE AND OFFLINE

In the world of sales and marketing, understanding how to apply the AIDA method in both online and offline channels is crucial to reaching a broad spectrum of potential customers and maximizing the impact of your strategies. This chapter explores how you can harmonize your actions between the two worlds, creating a cohesive and effective brand experience that guides the consumer through each step of the purchasing process, regardless of channel.

ATTENTION TO DIVERSIFIED CHANNELS

The first step of AIDA, capturing attention, can be achieved through a variety of channels.

- **Online:** Social media, SEO and paid advertising are powerful tools for capturing attention online. Each platform has its own set of best practices and formats that can be explored to reach your target audience.

- **Offline:** Traditional advertising like billboards, radio and TV are still effective in reaching a wide and diverse audience. Participation in events and sponsorships can also increase brand visibility.

MAINTAINING INTEREST

Maintaining customer interest requires relevant and engaging content, both online and offline.

- **Online:** Blogs, emails and social media are ideal platforms for providing content that educates, entertains and informs, maintaining interest over time.

- **Offline:** Printed materials such as brochures and newsletters, as well as workshops and seminars, can provide added value while maintaining your audience's interest.

CREATING DESIRE

Turning interest into desire requires a deep understanding of your customer's motivations and a compelling presentation of the benefits of your product or service.

- **Online:** Personalization and product recommendations based on online user behavior data can create a deeper connection and generate desire.

- **Offline:** Live product demonstrations, immersive in-store experiences or personalized service can be extremely effective in creating desire.

DRIVING TO ACTION

Action is the ultimate goal, and making this step easier for the customer is essential, whether online or offline.

- **Online:** Optimized checkouts, limited-time offers and clear CTAs on websites and e-commerce platforms are key to converting interest into purchase.

- **Offline:** Well-trained salespeople, exclusive in-store offers and easy payment options can effectively drive customers to action.

INTEGRATED STRATEGIES FOR GREATER IMPACT

The key to a successful cross-channel AIDA strategy is integration. Campaigns must be cohesive and complementary, ensuring that brand messages and values are consistent across all customer touchpoints.

- **Multichannel campaigns:** Develop campaigns that cross online and offline, reinforcing the brand message and gently guiding the customer from one AIDA stage to the next.

- **Analysis and adjustment:** Use data from both worlds to analyze performance, adjust strategies and optimize return on investment.

As we move on to " **RESOURCES TO DEEPEN YOUR AIDA KNOWLEDGE** ", it is essential to recognize that effectively applying the AIDA method, whether online, offline or through an integrated approach, requires a deep understanding of your target audience and an ability to adapt and personalize your strategies to meet your needs and preferences. Be ready to explore a range of resources that will deepen your understanding and ability to apply the AIDA method effectively to your own campaigns.

RESOURCES TO DEEPEN YOUR KNOWLEDGE

Mastering the AIDA method and applying it effectively in your marketing and sales strategies is a continuous process of learning and adaptation. Fortunately, there are a wide range of resources available to deepen your knowledge and refine your skills. This chapter offers a careful selection of resources that can enrich your understanding of AIDA and enhance your campaigns.

BOOKS

- **Influence : The Psychology of Persuasion , by Robert Cialdini :** Although not focused exclusively on AIDA, this classic provides fundamental insights into how people are persuaded, which is critical at every stage of AIDA.

- **Contagious : How to Build Word of Mouth in the Digital Age, by Jonah Berger :** Learn how to create content that captures attention and is shared widely, a key component of the Attention stage in AIDA.

- **Made to Stick: Why Some Ideas Survive and Others Die by Chip Heath and Dan Heath :** This book offers valuable strategies for making your messages memorable, helping to maintain interest and create desire.

ONLINE COURSES

- **Digital Marketing Specialization , on Coursera :** Offered by the University of Illinois, this course covers several facets of digital marketing, including how to capture attention and engage an audience online.

- **Marketing in a Digital World , on edX :** This course explores how digital tools transform marketing and can be used to implement the AIDA method effectively.

WORKSHOPS AND WEBINARS

- Attending workshops and webinars offered by industry leaders and educational institutions can provide up-to-date and practical insights into how AIDA is being applied in different sectors. Look for events that focus on emerging trends in digital marketing, consumer psychology and content strategies.

BLOGS AND PODCASTS

- **HubSpot Blog** : An excellent source of educational articles on all aspects of marketing and sales, including strategies for implementing AIDA.

- **Marketing Over Coffee** : A podcast that covers both traditional marketing tactics and the latest trends in digital marketing, offering insights applicable to AIDA.

ANALYSIS AND TESTING TOOLS

- Mastering the use of analytics tools like Google Analytics, as well as A/B testing platforms like Optimizely , is crucial for measuring the effectiveness of your AIDA strategies and adjusting your approaches based on real data.

NEXT STEPS

With these resources at your fingertips, you are well-equipped to further explore each aspect of the AIDA method and how it can be applied to improve your marketing and sales strategies. In the next chapter, " **30-DAY ACTION PLAN: IMPLEMENTING AIDA INTO YOUR SALES PROCESS** ," we'll provide a step-by-step guide to putting what you've learned into practice, helping you turn theory into action and ideas into measurable results. Get ready to dive into a practical plan that will structure your application of AIDA, ensuring you can start seeing tangible improvements in your marketing and sales campaigns.

30-DAY ACTION PLAN: IMPLEMENTING AIDA INTO YOUR SALES PROCESS

Effectively implementing the AIDA method into your marketing and sales strategies can transform customer engagement and boost conversions. This chapter offers a detailed 30-day action plan for integrating AIDA into your sales process, ensuring a structured approach that can be tailored to the specific needs of your business.

DAY 1-2: DEFINE YOUR TARGET AUDIENCE

- Conduct detailed research to clearly identify your target audience. Use demographic, psychographic, and behavioral data to create customer personas.

DAY 3-4: MAP THE CUSTOMER JOURNEY

- Understand how your target audience moves through the sales funnel. Identify key touchpoints and how the AIDA method applies at each stage.

DAY 5-7: PLAN SPECIFIC AIDA STRATEGIES

- Develop creative ideas to capture attention, generate interest, create desire and induce action. Plan campaigns that can be executed across different channels, both online and offline.

DAY 8-10: CREATE CONTENT TO CAPTURE ATTENTION

- Develop compelling visual content, catchy headlines, and persuasive messages designed to catch the attention of your target audience.

DAY 11-12: LAUNCH ATTENTION CAMPAIGNS

- Implement your attention campaigns using paid advertising, social media, SEO and other relevant channels.

DAY 13-15: MONITORING AND ADJUSTMENT

- Monitor the performance of your attention campaigns. Use analytics tools to adjust and optimize strategies as needed.

DAY 16-18: DEVELOP ENGAGING CONTENT

- Produce and distribute content that educates and informs your audience, such as blog articles, e-books, and webinars, to maintain interest.

DAY 19-20: ENGAGEMENT STRATEGIES

- Implement interactive strategies, such as quizzes and polls, to increase customer engagement.

DAY 21-22: EVALUATION AND OPTIMIZATION

- Review engagement metrics. Make adjustments to strategies to improve customer interest and engagement.

DAY 23-24: CREATE PERSONALIZED OFFERS

- Use customer data to create personalized offers that speak directly to your needs, increasing desire.

DAY 25-26: DEMONSTRATIONS AND SOCIAL PROOF

- Implement product demos and share testimonials and case studies to strengthen desire for your product or service.

DAY 27: DESIRE ANALYSIS

- Evaluate the effectiveness of your strategies in creating desire. Adjust your approach based on the feedback and data you collect.

DAY 28-29: MAKE PURCHASING EASIER

- Simplify the purchasing process and implement clear and attractive CTAs. Offer incentives, like limited-time discounts or special offers, to encourage action.

DAY 30: FINAL ASSESSMENT AND ADJUSTMENTS

- Review the overall performance of AIDA campaigns. Identify areas of success and those in need of improvement.

Plan your next steps to refine and expand your AIDA strategies.

This 30-day plan is just the beginning. Implementing the AIDA method in your sales process is a continuous cycle of learning, testing and optimizing. Use the insights gained during this month to refine your approaches, explore new strategies, and continue to build deeper relationships with your customers. With dedication and adaptation, the AIDA method can become a powerful tool in your marketing and sales arsenal, boosting customer engagement and taking your conversions to new heights.

As we turn the final page of this journey together, I sincerely hope that the learnings shared here have touched your heart and sparked new perspectives. If this book has brought you any value, I kindly ask that you take a few moments to leave a review on Amazon. Your words not only help me grow and hone my craft, but they also guide other readers in their quests for knowledge and inspiration. Your opinion is a valuable gift, both for me and for the community of readers looking for stories that transform. I sincerely thank you for sharing this journey with me and I hope we can meet again in the pages of a new adventure.

REGINALDO OSNILDO

Hello, I'm Reginaldo Osnildo, author and innovator in the areas of sales, technology, and communication strategies. My experience ranges from the academic environment, as a professor and researcher at the University of Southern Santa Catarina, to practice as a strategist at Grupo Catarinense de Rádios. With a PhD in sales narratives and digital convergence, and a master's degree in storytelling and social imaginary, I bring my readers a unique fusion of theory and practice. My goal is to provide knowledge in a simple, practical and didactic language, encouraging direct application in personal and professional life.

Yours sincerely

Reginaldo Osnildo

+55 48 991913865

reginaldoosnildo@gmail.com